In Between

Written by Barrie Wade
Illustrated by Bruce Ingman

Collins Educational
An imprint of HarperCollinsPublishers

Contents

What I Think

TRUTH 4
SHY 6
CLOAKROOM 8
PRAYER BEFORE PARENTS' EVENING 10

Our Own Work

PLANEMAKERS 14
CRYSTALS 16
WEATHER OR NOT 18

Great Attraction

FIGHT 22
CONKERS 24
COMING FIRST 26
DELIBERATE INTENT 28

Dreadful Moments

MARKING TIME 30
NIGHTMARE 32
SWIMMING LESSON 34
NAME-CALLING 36

A Helping Hand

A BORN TEACHER 38
LIKE THE CLAPPERS 40
SECOND THOUGHTS 42

Older Now

THE COLLECTOR 44
IN BETWEEN 46

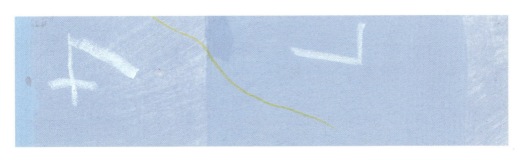

What I Think

TRUTH

Sticks and stones may break my bones,
but words can also hurt me.
Stones and sticks break only skin,
while words are ghosts that haunt me.

Slant and curved the word-swords fall
to pierce and stick inside me.
Bats and bricks may ache through bones,
but words can mortify me.

Pain from words has left its scar
on mind and heart that's tender.
Cuts and bruises now have healed;
it's words that I remember.

SHY

It's not fair
when folks stare
and everybody knows
my face goes
red as a lollipop
on the top
of a stick.

    I flinch on
    the mention
    of names in assembly,
    go trembly
    as cobwebs on ceilings:
    the feeling's
    horrific.

How I hate
to come late
and to apologise
with all eyes
on the flame of my face:
the disgrace
lights my wick.

    I don't put
    my hand up
    to questions in class, though
    I do know
    the answers and don't care
    if teacher
    thinks I'm thick.

I'm not keen
to be seen
on the boards of the stage
and engage
in creative drama:
the trauma
makes me sick

and it's worse
to rehearse
in the choir, for I've tried.
Really I'd
love to be confident
but I can't
learn the trick.

    I detest
    any jest
    or joke about me, try
    not to cry
    as my inside deflates
    when my mates
    take the Mick.

Like a worm
I will turn.
One day when I'm older
and bolder
I'll give famous speeches
and cheek all the teachers,
make horrible screeches
and bring nasty creatures,
then keep out of reach as
they all bite,
claw and fight,
scratch and kick.

CLOAKROOM

Anoraks hang limp and folded,
bats sleeping by day;

      when steam rises from racked rows
      they are kippers to be smoked.

These pipes are comfort from bullies,
hot and final sanctuary,

      and the best place in hide and seek
      is hanging crucifixed

across two pegs with knees drawn up
beneath a duffle coat.

      I hid once through assembly,
      the piano mirage faint

and singing voices lapping
at some distant shore.

      My teacher found me drowsed by rain forests
      steaming under tropic sun.

      She was kind and simply asked
      why I was late.

      I don't recall my answer, only that
      my mind had drained

      to rows of empty question marks
      turned upside-down.

PRAYER BEFORE PARENTS' EVENING

Miss, guide my fingers with this decimal.
I know that with your help it's possible
To put the point into its proper place
And avoid mathematical disgrace.

At last I think that I have found the trick
Of mental problems in arithmetic.
I've noticed everybody sits like me
Hiding their calculator on their knee.

Miss, protect me from these hard subtractions
And from the tricks of complicated fractions.
At the mere mention of denominator
My brain goes mushy like a mashed potato.

Miss, I know how hard you have been trying,
But I need more help with multiplying.
I know that eight times nine is seventy four,
But why should nine times eight be seven more?

My father says that I should try things out,
But you should have heard my mother shout
About that carpet. I've grown warier
Of any work to do with area

And I've nearly given up with problem maths.
I shudder at the thought of filling baths
Ever since our kitchen ceiling dripped with rain.
I daren't experiment like that again.

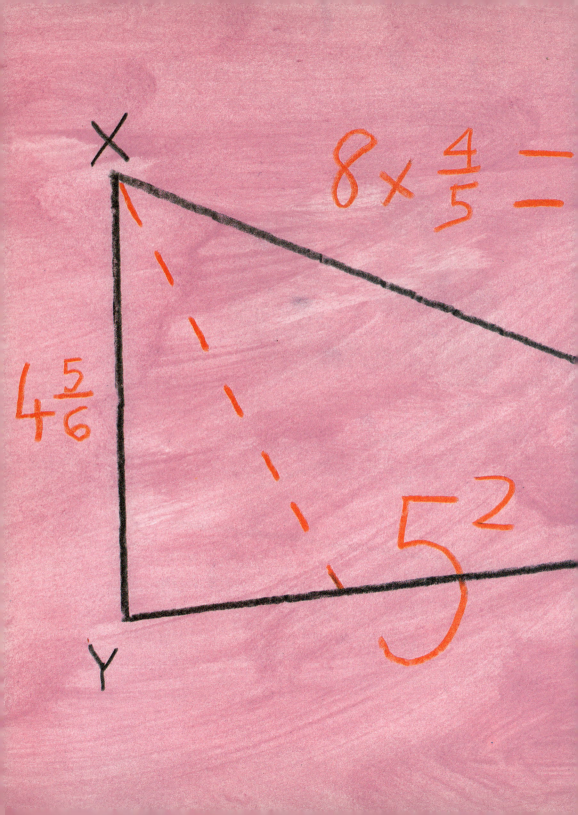

Since I have not discovered what's the use
Of making squares on a hypotenuse,
Pythagoras is so much Greek to me.
I'm sinking in the swamp of geometry.

Miss, I start out with the best intentions,
But I'm even worse in three dimensions –
So my father says. We're all agreed on
The importance of the polyhedron:

I take the utmost care to use my rule
And cut card straight, but, Miss, I'm such a fool
With glue that, always when it's time to hang
Them up, mine sags just like a squashed meringue.

My father says that there are some things worse
Ahead – that's algebra and calculus
And something that he calls equations.
The names alone bring palpitations.

So guide me through the wilderness ahead.
Arrange to have right answers in my head,
But, if you find it's too impractical
To give me knowledge mathematical,

Then let my mother come to realise
I try, though numbers swim before my eyes,
To be the brainchild that will suit her
And that I can't be a computer.

Our Own Work

PLANEMAKERS

Our silver polyhedrons spin
slowly overhead:
gliders climbing classroom thermals.

All our own work: we fashioned joints,
glued every section,
spread the shiny paint,

hung them in threaded
squadrons underneath
a cloudless ceiling.

We began with cube and cuboid,
trainer pyramids
and single-engined cones.

Now expert, we construct and name
octahedron bombers
and transport dodecahedrons.

Silver flashes from the waggled wings
of Spitfire and Hurricane
returning safely.

Bunkered at our desks,
our hearts respond with victory rolls
of reflected glory.

CRYSTALS

First, in saucers we spread salt.
Our imagination turns

        its shimmer into spoil heaps
      drawn from far-off diamond mines

beneath the tawny plain
of Africa. We hold this dream

        until the drench of water
          vanquishes their fire.

A string of disappearing pools,
we range them along windowsills

    and the sun steals in on lion's paws
        to lap away their drink.

Our teacher mixes 'poison'
in a glass apart for safety;

      it attracts us like a blinding sky
        of fierce, ice-shattering blue.

Our waterholes days later
have dried up to brittle crusts

        of sharp-edged crystals
      glittering like splintered glass.

Ice-wonder fills our eyes
almost to snow-blinding.

        Our teacher's soft brown hand
          shows diamonds of blue

deeper than sky or sea.
Her eyes sparkle ice and fire.

WEATHER OR NOT

If it rains in the afternoon, we'll hold it in the morning.

Our school's had three wet sports days on the trot,
three days when you could better sail a yacht
around our field and dress in warm windcheaters
than strip to paddle-splash a hundred metres.
Miss Price said, "Oh, this isn't very jolly,"
peering out from underneath her brolly
and we said that it wasn't fair
that *she* was dry when we had soaking hair
and, if *she* had to run, she'd feel as sick as
us with *her* vest tucked inside *her* knickers.

She must have taken what we said to heart
because the weekend after was the start
when our Miss Price began to be expert
at rain. We saw her hitching up her skirt
and peddling past our house on Saturday.
We didn't know that she was on her way
to school or, as her creaky bike tore past,
that she was thinking of her weather forecast.

Our climate education, stopped at weathercocks,
was launched on Monday by Miss Price's painted box,
the kind our school had never seen before.
It had a little, slatted, louvre door,
was fixed upon a pole next to the drive
and looked exactly like a white beehive,
while next to it, standing like an open drain,
was a funnel-like can for catching the rain.

With pride Miss Price introduced it to us,
showed us how to take the temperatures,
measure the speed of wind and depth of rain
and promised us that never again
would sports day be so wet and painful
once we had mastered trends in rainfall.

Our school-lives now became less troublesome
bounded by minimum and maximum
and figures that we carried to her
on wind and rain and temperature.
She kept us working like automata
on readings from the new barometer.
The coloured graphs we made were all dramatic
and the figures seemed to make her go ecstatic.
She always found our charts exciting
and forgot to give us so much writing.

Every Monday morning she would greet us
with the weekend fall in millimetres
or in the playground she would come at us
with latest news from her thermometers,
and she could sense, as if she'd radar,
when dogs sniffed round her precious rain jar.
She shoo-ed them off each time they sported
in case her rainfall data got distorted.

So in this way without apology
we all were plunged in meteorology.
Whether we learned or not, there is no doubt of it
that something great at last came out of it,
for Miss Price chose the day for sports this year
and on the day she got a kind of cheer,
a bit like ice-cubes rattling together,
since we blamed her for bringing weather
that we had never had before in June
and quite unlike the previous year's monsoon.
We'll not forget that sporting episode.
It never rained at all, but how it snowed!

Great Attraction

FIGHT

"A scrap! A scrap!"
The tingle in the scalp
starts us running.

The shout drains
our playground just as though
a plug was pulled

here in the space
in which two twisted, furious
bodies writhe.

Rules will not prise
these savages apart.
No ref will interpose

with shouts of "Break!"
This contest has one single,
vicious round

of grab and grapple,
wrestle, thump and scrabble,
flail and scratch.

We take no sides.
Our yells are wolves howling
for blood of any kind.

Our fingers clench.
The thrill claws in our throats
like raging thirst.

The whistle shrills
and splits our pack. The circle
heaves and shatters.

The fighters still
are blind and deaf, won't hear
or see until,

parted, they go limp
as cubs drawn by the scruff
from some hot lair.

Now they are tame.
Standing outside Sir's room
grinning their shame.

Chastened, we feel
the snarls of wildness
stifle in us.

CONKERS

Out of sight they spend whole summers
growing spiky in the leaf corners.
We never hear them drop:
their swell and fall
is secret as imagination.
In split shells they lie,

nuggets for polishing.
Damp from casings briefly clings
like mist across the sunrise.
They burnish in our hands,
send bubbles through the blood,
make minds molten with joy.

They are poems, varied
and irresistible,
each containing
its own new germination.
Arranging them on strings
will thread our Autumn through with fire.

COMING FIRST

Like a vixen with a sense of purpose
I come first to school, sniffing cool air

    with the piece of slate I carry
    warmed inside my palm.

Our hopscotch paving stones are wrapped
by silver crossed in ribbons:

    in front of me, in damp and dark,
    shy snails have trailed their patterns.

My aim is certain. Missing all the cracks,
my feet are delicate as paws.

    When the gang comes, I'll be forced away
    so clumsy legs can trip and stumble

over slender prints already laid
before their brutal day began to warm.

    I'll keep these patterns in my head intact
    as damp dries on the outside of our classroom wall.

DELIBERATE INTENT

Dogs I don't mind. They sniff
a leg then trot away,
but cats can smell my allergy.
They make for me deliberately.

They rub against my leg
or lie in wait to pounce.
The only thing I know is that
my lap is heaven for a cat.

Some drift like smoke
then give a sudden leap
to sit with claws clamped on my knee
and seem to smile their victory.

My eyelids scald and itch.
Tears trickle down my cheeks.
"No, really I am not upset.
It's just that I can't stand your pet."

Dreadful Moments

MARKING TIME

Of all the dreadful times I hate
it most when Miss marks English books here
at her desk. How can I concentrate
on silent reading when my hair

crawls with fear. I know the hobbit
that I drew is smeared and scratchy –
more like Smaug. I'd like to grab it
from the pile except she'd catch me

long before I reached the door. Sweat breaks
its sticky showers in my hands.
Under lidded eyes I watch the marks
her neat pen makes. I hope she understands

my felt-tips cannot be controlled
by spell or curse (I've tried). It's hardly possible
some grey-haired wizard would give gold
elven rings to magic me invisible –

though now I need one most. That book
is mine! The hobbit upside down
looks even more like Smaug. I look
away in case I see that frown

crinkle her brow. Oh, no! "Stop work,"
she says, "and look this way." I'll die!
All eyes are arrows at my book
piercing its weak spot. Dragon cry

of agony starts deep down in my chest
until Miss smiles, as lovely as Galadriel:
"I want to show you this – by far the best."
I might begin to trust in magic after all.

NIGHTMARE

At night I sometimes lie imagining
worse spectres than the lidded dark can bring.

My thoughts shape monster, ghoul and devil
whose first heartstopping crunch on gravel

stifles every scream for help inside my room
as they were echoes prisoned in a tomb.

Sly spectres through my wide eyesockets creep
where I am trapped within the skull of sleep.

Here stalks that demon with the human face
that makes me lurch and tumble down through space

or wildly run and yet stay fixed in terror
while his pursuing beasts draw ever nearer.

I feel their burning eyes and glistening tongues
but wake before the sinking of their fangs

to find my body stiffened from the chase
and mask of horror frozen on my face.

I know I can't be coffined in my grave
because live fear goes jangling down each nerve

and on my skin the sweat clings cool
as scum upon the surface of a pool.

Then gradually I sail the velvet lakes of sleep
and let no ripple stir the monsters of the deep.

SWIMMING LESSON

It never happened –
only whirlpool fear
spun my thoughts until
they drowned in water
colder than the ice-
floes loose in Arctic seas.

My whitened hands clung
at the metal rail,
bleak with hopelessness,
as other hands might slip
on life-belt ropes cast
on some leaden surface.

The teachers left me
leeched against the side.
They hadn't heard the bully
say he'd duck my head
and yet they understood
the rigid clasp of fear.

Rising steam was mist
of death descending
and my mind had gone
senseless as waste cod
shipped off a fishing boat
to bob upon the tide.

It never happened –
for the bully quite
forgot. His plunges
shivered my gooseflesh
from the deeper end.
At last we clambered out.

It never happened –
only in my mind –
but swimming lessons
still stretch nets of fear
whose threads cling like smell
of chlorine on my skin.

NAME-CALLING

I once called out to Doreen Vickers,
"Hey, Doreen! Have you lost your knickers?"
She didn't give a real reply,
but simply looked me in the eye

and swept right past me, walking like a queen
all regal-like and so serene.
It couldn't be she hadn't heard,
because I'd shouted every word.

I really hate to be ignored.
Next day I wrote upon the board,
'Doreen Vickers wets her knickers',
then collapsed in grins and snickers,

until Miss asked me what was wrong.
I'm sure she well knew all along
for without turning she exclaimed,
"Geoffrey, I would like the blackboard cleaned!"

I couldn't giggle any more,
but bent my head towards the floor.
Feeling the fire of all those eyes,
I walked up to collect the prize

of shame – in silence tighter strained
than skin upon balloons. Fun drained
away, the tightness grew and burst
behind my eyes. I blame the dust

cloud that the blackboard rubber made.
I tell you, you'd be much dismayed
to find the fun of calling names
explodes when nobody complains.

A Helping Hand

A BORN TEACHER

Yethterday I thtarted with my brayth.
The dentith thaid it ith nothing
but a plathtic plate that thtretcheth
thilver wire acroth my teeth.

It ith thuppothed to thtraighten them,
but yethterday it thtopped me thinking
and I theldom thpoke.
It wath filling my mouth all night.

At breakfatht I got Ryth Krithpith
thtuck underneath the plathtic plate
and Mum thaid girlth who thtick fingerth
inthide their mouths are not nyth.

Thank goodneth that my Grandad comth
to our houth on Thaturdayth
and he ith wyth and underthtandth.
He thayth I thimply need to practith.

He knowth all about teeth
thinth all of hith are plathtic
and he keepth them in a glath
bethide hith bed at night.

He thtarted me on thalted crithpth
and by the thecond bag my tongue
could thweep the thticky piethth off
before they thwam underneath and got thtuck.

Then we had thpeaking ectherthytheth.
Thoon I could thpeak and not thpray.
Grandad lykth my thilver thmile.
He thayth it maykth me much more beautiful.

He ecthplained how no-one could have been
more beautiful than Grandma dethpite
thith mark upon her cheek.
He thaid that Grandma even darkened it
to draw attention to her lovely fayth.
'Highlighting' he called it.
Her photo may be blurred
but anyone can thee the darkened thpot.

Now I know I will talk perfectly by Monday
and that my grin will then be nearly permanent.
Yeth, my Grandad ith a born teacher.
We could do with more like him.

LIKE THE CLAPPERS

The rich kid at the big house lives
with windows barred and shutters
that swing tight closed at night
and iron railings black as spears.

They don't let him out for exercise
even when his mother drags her poodles out,
but sometimes you can hear him
playing piano scales – never tunes.

I picture him padding out his room
in carpetslipper figure-eights,
crossing days off a glossy calendar
until he is released to boarding school.

I clench a stick into my fist,
ride my bike along his pavement
and rattle down his railing cage,
then shoot off like the clappers.

It's the best that I can do
for sympathy – that sound
like friendship rattled
in a hundred separate cells.

SECOND THOUGHTS

This was the house for knock
and run. I only did it once
and then a cruel clattering
and twitch of yellow curtain
haunted me for days and hung
like lead around my neck.

        This is the house with paint that peels
        and seeded grasses in the lawn
        with dusty windows spider-webbed
        where his fist has thumped at children,
        nurses, dogs, home-helps – all
        but me and meals on wheels.

                This is the house where next I
                knocked and waited paralysed
                while the shuffling came close,
                where the old door gave a creak,
                where I shouted, "Can I make your tea?"
                and where he answered gently, "Aye."

Older Now

THE COLLECTOR

"...and do you collect anything?"
Usually it's some new adult
making kidtalk to be polite
and certain every child collects

something or other – coins or cards,
bottles, badges, leaves or labels,
foreign stamps or dolls. To admit
collecting is to stay a child

and so I always answer 'no'
(which is, in any case, the truth)
and watch the sudden swerve and dive
of conversation startled off.

I have treasures not to speak of:
straight cockpheasant quills and oil-pooled
peacock feathers, one tiled woodcock wing,
the bleached bone of a gannet beak.

No, I do not collect bird bits.
In fact, I keep them separate
and you would call it 'separation'
if you could ever understand.

Only in awkward passages
of conversation do they merge,
startle and stutter, swerve and glide,
then swoop brilliant and deadly.

IN BETWEEN

I have reached the age
of no more birthday parties.
For a year or two my friends
have eaten cake and icing
only not to give offence.
I'm told that I am far too young
for parties that my sister goes to.
I have a front door key as recompense
and am allowed to come from school
first in the darkening, empty house.

I freeze like statues in the hall,
grope for the lightswitch, blind as buff,
play hunt-the-kettle's-lid then, while
it sings, have choice of every kitchen chair.
Alone I can experiment
with crisp and cornflake sandwich cake
without the candles on of course,
drink my tea remembering the brief
exploding fizz of Pepsi tops released
and, although I know my mother's tread upon the path,

I can pretend it is the postman's knock.

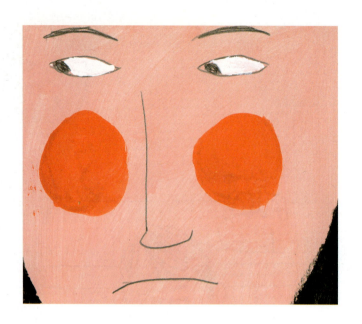

The aliens are out to hurt the players from Planet Earth!

Wow! Unfair tackle. Foul, ref! Red card!

The player groans with pain. It should be at least a yellow card, but there is no whistle from the ref!

But then the chance is snatched away when the alien keeper spits a ball of fire at him!

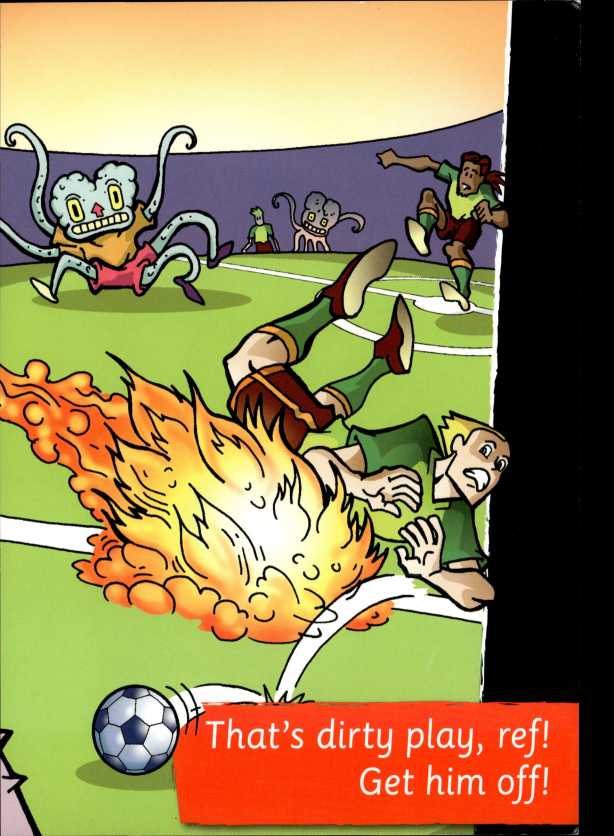

The striker falls to the ground, holding his head in anger.

'What am I doing playing in this game?' he asks. 'This is extreme football!'

There are no rules other than the Alien ones! They make them up as they go along. United are in control!

They seem to be everywhere with their squid-like legs, kicking the players as well as the ball!

They race back up the field and shoot hard for goal.

The defenders dive for cover, but Planet Earth's keeper remains standing. He is determined to stop it getting in the net.

But what's this? What's happening under the keeper's feet?

The ref finally blows the whistle for full time! It is the only thing he has done right all afternoon.

The Earth players are crushed and dazed. They cannot work out what is going on!

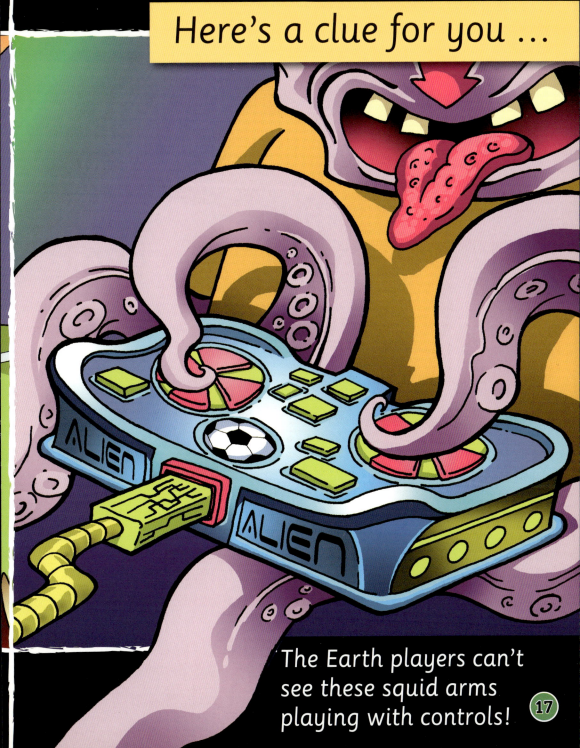

So what was all that about?

Here's a clue for you …

The Earth players can't see these squid arms playing with controls!

 Matt: What a game, Amba!

 Amba: It's a pleasure to be here, Matt.

 Matt: So it's three-all with five minutes to play. Can one side still win it?

 Amba: Oh yes, I think there are more goals to come, for sure!

Matt: We've seen two hat-tricks in this game so far.

First Nicky Cole put United three up …

 Amba: ... and then Shane Nixon drew Athletico level. The wild child walks the walk!

So yes, three-all.

 Amba: That was a stupid foul. It's a penalty! This is a real danger for Athletico.

 Matt: The whistle blows, and Cole takes the pen!

 Amba: Keeper Foster dives … Wow! What a save!

 Amba: A quick goal kick and United are caught upfield. Lucas whips in a cross ... and it's 4-3 to Athletico!

 Matt: Nixon flew through the air there. That's his fourth in this game. And it was a glancing header to treasure!

 Matt: Let's go to Sue Lane now.

 Sue: Well there's just three extra minutes added on …

Sue Lane SC LIVE

Sue: It's very tense down here. United's French boss is not happy.

Anton: Three minutes! Come on! We can still win this. Attack!

Sue: The two managers are squaring up. This could get nasty. I'm amazed; they've both lost it!

Peter: Don't you push me! We will win this game!

Anton: Shut up! Don't you tell me what to do!

Matt: The referee has sent them both to the stand. I've never seen anything like it!

 Matt: Now the ball runs loose and … GOAL! United save it with the last kick of the game.

 Amba: What can I say? What a match!

Sue: So it looks like you two are friends again!

Anton: Of course. The game is over.

Peter: Honours even! It was a magic match!